Monsoo

Written by Saaleh Patel

Collins

a wet backpack

a red raincoat

a wet backpack

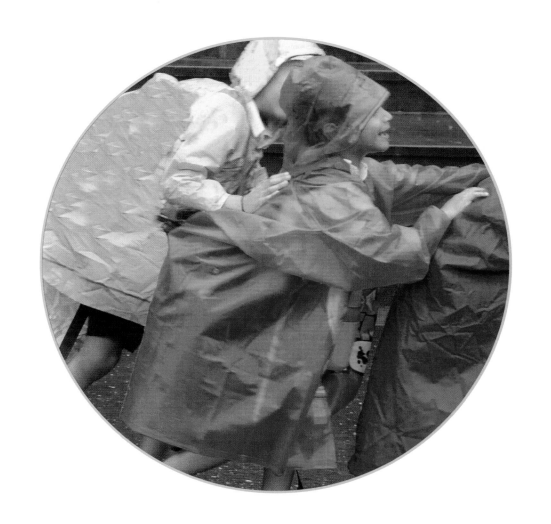

a red raincoat

a wooden boat

a pink helmet

a wooden boat

a pink helmet

a farmer in the rain

fantastic cow horns

a farmer in the rain

fantastic cow horns

🐾 Review: After reading 🐾

Use your assessment from hearing the children read to choose any GPCs, words or tricky words that need additional practice.

Read 1: Decoding

- Use grapheme cards to make any words you need to practise. Model reading those words, using teacher-led blending.
- Ask the children to follow as you read the whole book, demonstrating fluency and prosody.

Read 2: Vocabulary

- Look back through the book and discuss the pictures. Encourage the children to talk about details that stand out for them. Use a dialogic talk model to expand on their ideas and recast them in full sentences as naturally as possible.
- Work together to expand vocabulary by naming objects in the pictures that children do not know.
- Look at page 11 and focus on the meaning of **fantastic**. Ask: Why do you think the horns are fantastic? (e.g. *they are big and painted in bright colours*)

Read 3: Comprehension

- Ask the children how they feel about rain, and why. Ask: Do you like to play in the rain? What special clothes do you wear in the rain? Explain that the monsoon is a time when there is a lot of rain in a part of the world (southern Asia).
- Turn to page 6 and talk about why the people need a wooden boat. Discuss how lots of rain has caused a flood.
- Reread pages 10 and 11 and talk about what the farmer and the cows are doing. Discuss how rain is important for growing crops.
- Turn to pages 14 and 15. Using the pictures as prompts, ask the children to explain what they have learned about the monsoon. Encourage them to back up their views with details from the book. Ask: What do people wear in the monsoon? Is there a lot of rain or a little bit of rain? Is it light or heavy rain?